Gooseberry Patch

gingerbread

Classics

Run! Run! As fast as you can!
You can't catch me,
I'm the gingerbread man!
–Old folktale

Easiest-Ever Gingerbread Boys

18-1/2 oz. pkg. spice
   cake mix
1 c. all-purpose flour
2 t. ground ginger

2 eggs, beaten
1/3 c. oil
1/2 c. molasses

Combine cake mix, flour and ginger in a large bowl; stir with a fork until blended. Mix in remaining ingredients. Beat with an electric mixer on medium speed for 2 minutes. Cover and refrigerate for 2 hours. Place dough on a floured surface; roll out to 1/4-inch thickness using a floured rolling pin. Cut out with cookie cutters as desired; place on greased baking sheets. Bake at 375 degrees for 8 to 10 minutes, until edges start to darken. Let cool on baking sheets for 5 minutes; remove to wire racks to cool completely. Makes 2 to 3 dozen.

Gingerbread is a holiday favorite! Bake up a batch of decorated gingerbread boys & girls and hot glue to a straw wreath form. Wind ribbon between the cookies and top with holly and a homespun bow.

Grandma's Gingersnaps

3/4 c. butter, softened
1 c. sugar
1 egg, beaten
1/2 c. molasses
2 T. fresh ginger, peeled
    and grated

2 c. all-purpose flour
2 t. baking soda
1/2 t. salt
1 T. cinnamon
Garnish: additional sugar

Blend butter and sugar in a large mixing bowl; add egg, blending until fluffy. Mix in molasses and ginger; set aside. Combine flour, baking soda, salt and cinnamon in another mixing bowl; stir into butter mixture. Shape dough into one-inch balls; roll in additional sugar and arrange on lightly greased baking sheets. Bake at 350 degrees for 10 to 12 minutes. Cool on wire racks. Makes about 4 dozen.

Ginger comes in several different forms...ground, crystallized and fresh. For best results, use the kind specified in a recipe, but in a pinch, 1/4 teaspoon ground ginger equals one tablespoon sliced fresh ginger root equals 1/4 cup minced crystallized ginger.

Moravian Spice Crisps

3/4 c. all-purpose flour
1/2 t. baking powder
1/4 t. baking soda
1/4 t. salt
1/2 t. cinnamon
1/2 t. white pepper

1/2 t. ground ginger
1/4 t. ground cloves
1/3 c. light brown sugar, packed
3 T. butter, softened
1/4 c. light molasses

Combine flour, baking powder, baking soda, salt and spices; set aside. Combine brown sugar and butter in a mixing bowl; beat with an electric mixer at low speed until blended; beat on high speed until creamy, about 2 minutes. Blend in molasses at medium speed. Stir in flour mixture with a spoon. Drop by rounded teaspoonfuls, about 4-inches apart, on greased baking sheets. Flatten each into a 2-inch circle. Bake at 350 degrees for 8 to 10 minutes. Let cool several minutes; remove to a wire rack to cool completely. Store in a tightly covered container. Makes about 3 dozen.

Make a gift bag for someone who loves to bake! Fill plastic zipping bags with the dry ingredients for your favorite gingerbread cookies. Tuck in a fun cookie cutter, a wooden spoon, colored sprinkles and your recipe!

Swedish Pepparkakor

1-1/2 c. butter, softened
2-1/4 c. sugar, divided
2 eggs, beaten
1/2 c. molasses
4 c. all-purpose flour

2 t. baking soda
1/2 t. salt
1 T. ground ginger
1-1/2 t. ground cloves
1-1/2 t. cinnamon

Blend together butter and 2 cups sugar in a medium bowl;
add eggs and molasses, mixing well. Stir in flour, baking soda,
salt and spices to make a stiff dough, adding more flour if
necessary. Roll out on a floured surface, 1/8-inch to 1/4-inch
thick. Cut out with cookie cutters as desired; arrange on
greased baking sheets. Sprinkle with remaining sugar. Bake
at 350 degrees for 5 to 6 minutes, until lightly golden. Makes
5 to 6 dozen.

Use a smaller cookie cutter to create a cut-out inside
a cookie. Fill the cut-out with crushed hard candy before
baking. As it bakes and melts, the candy magically
creates a stained-glass look.

★ Classics ★

Gingerbread Coffee Cake

1 c. molasses	1 T. baking powder
1 c. water	1 t. cinnamon
1 t. baking soda	1/4 t. ground ginger
1/2 c. butter, softened	1/4 t. ground cloves
1 c. brown sugar, packed	Garnish: Powdered Sugar
2 eggs, beaten	Glaze (page 29)
2 c. all-purpose flour	

Bring molasses and water to a boil in a small saucepan;
stir in baking soda. Cool. Beat butter, brown sugar and eggs
in a medium bowl; set aside. Combine flour, baking powder
and spices in another bowl; beat one-half at a time, alternately
with molasses mixture, into butter mixture until well mixed.
Pour into a greased 13"x9" baking pan; sprinkle with Walnut
Topping. Bake at 350 degrees for 40 minutes. Drizzle with
Powdered Sugar Glaze while still warm. Serves 12 to 15.

Walnut Topping:

1/3 c. all-purpose flour	1/2 t. cinnamon
1/3 c. sugar	1/2 t. ground ginger
1/3 c. chopped walnuts	3 T. butter

Combine all ingredients except butter. Cut in butter with a
pastry blender until coarsely crumbled.

*Molasses is used in many gingerbread recipes. Unless
specified, you can use dark molasses for full flavor
or light molasses for a milder taste.*

Gingerbread Creamer Mix

2 c. powdered non-dairy creamer	1/2 t. allspice
	1/2 t. ground cloves
1/2 c. brown sugar, packed	1/4 t. ground ginger
1 t. cinnamon	1/4 t. nutmeg

Combine all ingredients in an airtight container; mix well.
Seal tightly and attach instructions. Makes about 2-3/4 cups.

Instructions:

Pour one heaping tablespoonful of mix into a mug of
hot coffee or tea. Stir to dissolve. Makes one serving.

Fill a pretty sugar bowl with Gingerbread Creamer Mix
and tie on a dainty silver spoon...a thoughtful gift
for any occasion.

Gingerbread Fruitcake Cookies

14-oz. pkg. gingerbread mix
6 T. water
1/4 c. butter, melted
4-oz. container candied
    orange peel, chopped

1/2 c. golden raisins
1/2 c. chopped pecans
1-1/2 c. powdered sugar
2-1/2 T. lemon juice
    or orange juice

Combine gingerbread mix, water and butter, stirring until smooth. Fold in orange peel, raisins and pecans. Drop dough by rounded teaspoonfuls onto lightly greased baking sheets. Bake at 350 degrees for 10 minutes. Let cool slightly on baking sheets; remove to wire racks to cool completely. Combine powdered sugar and lemon or orange juice, stirring until smooth. Drizzle over cooled cookies. Makes 4 dozen.

Glass apothecary jars are big and roomy...ideal for holding a growing collection of cookie cutters!

Ginger Pennies

1 c. brown sugar, packed
1 egg, beaten
1/4 c. blackstrap molasses
3/4 c. butter, softened
1-1/2 c. all-purpose flour

1/2 t. baking soda
1/4 t. salt
3/4 t. ground ginger
3/4 t. cinnamon
1/2 t. ground cloves

Blend brown sugar, egg, molasses and butter in a medium bowl; set aside. Mix together flour, baking soda, salt and spices; beat into brown sugar mixture. Spoon batter into a gallon-size plastic zipping bag; snip off a small corner. Pipe small dots (about 1/8 teaspoon or a 1-1/2 inch mound) one-inch apart on greased baking sheets. Bake at 325 degrees for 3 minutes. Immediately remove from baking sheets onto wire racks; let cool. Can be stored in an airtight container for several months. Makes 10 to 12 dozen.

Hand deliver edible Christmas cards this year.
Just cut gingerbread into postcard-size pieces,
bake and pipe on holiday wishes with royal icing...top
off with gumdrops and candy canes!

Apple Gingerbread Squares

1/4 c. butter
1/3 c. molasses
1/3 c. brown sugar, packed
1/2 c. orange juice
1 egg, beaten
1-1/4 c. all-purpose flour
1 t. baking soda
1 t. cinnamon

1 t. ground ginger
1/4 t. ground cloves
1/4 t. salt
1 Golden Delicious apple,
   cored, peeled and
   chopped
Optional: powdered sugar

Melt butter in a medium saucepan over medium heat. Add molasses, brown sugar and orange juice; whisk until blended. Remove from heat; stir in egg. Combine flour, baking soda, spices and salt; stir into molasses mixture just until combined. Stir in apple. Pour into a greased and floured 8"x8" baking pan; bake at 350 degrees for 25 to 30 minutes, or until center is firm. Cut into squares; sprinkle with powdered sugar, if desired. Serve warm. Makes 8 servings.

No time to frost your gingerbread? Just top with a stencil and gently dust with powdered sugar or glittery sanding sugar...beautiful!

Ginger & Spice & Everything Nice Muffin Mix

1-3/4 c. all-purpose flour
2 T. sugar
1 T. baking powder
1/2 t. baking soda
1/2 t. salt

1/2 t. vanilla powder
1 t. cinnamon
1/2 t. nutmeg
1/4 t. ground ginger
1/4 t. ground cloves

Combine ingredients; place in an airtight container. Copy instruction tag below; attach to container. Makes one dozen.

Ginger & Spice & Everything Nice

MUFFIN MIX

Combine muffin mix with 1/4 cup melted butter, 1 egg and 1 cup milk; stir until just moistened. Fill greased or paper-lined muffin tins 2/3 full of batter; bake at 400° for 15 minutes. Makes 12.

Gingerbread Brownies

1-1/2 c. all-purpose flour
1 c. sugar
1/2 t. baking soda
1/4 c. baking cocoa
1 t. ground ginger
1 t. allspice

1 t. cinnamon
1/2 t. ground cloves
1/4 c. butter, melted
1/3 c. molasses
2 eggs, beaten

Combine flour, sugar, baking soda, cocoa and spices in a large mixing bowl; mix well. Blend in butter, molasses and eggs; mix well. Spread in a greased 13"x9" baking pan; bake at 350 degrees for 20 minutes. Cool on a wire rack; cut into bars. Makes 2 dozen.

Don't forget icy milk is perfect with gingerbread!
Serve it up in a new vintage-style milk bottle...what a
fun "remember when" memory.

Butterscotch Gingerbread Cut-Outs

1/2 c. butter, softened
1/2 c. brown sugar, packed
3.4-oz. pkg. cook & serve
   butterscotch pudding mix
1 egg, beaten
1-1/2 c. all-purpose flour

1/2 t. baking soda
1-1/2 t. ground ginger
1 t. cinnamon
Optional: Powdered Sugar
   Frosting (page 29),
   colored sugars

Blend together butter, brown sugar and pudding mix in a medium bowl; mix well. Beat in egg; stir in remaining ingredients. Chill until slightly firm. Roll out 1/4 to 1/2-inch thick on a lightly floured surface; cut out with cookie cutters. Arrange on greased baking sheets; bake at 350 degrees for 10 to 12 minutes. Decorate as desired. Makes one to 2 dozen.

Decorate the Christmas tree with fresh-baked gingerbread boys & girls! Before baking, use a drinking straw to make a hole at the top of each. Thread a ribbon through the holes to hang up cookies.

Dutch Speculaas

3 c. all-purpose flour	1 c. butter
1/8 t. baking powder	1-1/4 c. light brown sugar,
1/8 t. salt	packed
1-1/2 t. cinnamon	1 egg
1 t. ground cloves	1/2 c. blanched almonds,
1 t. ground ginger	finely ground

Stir together flour, baking powder, salt and spices; set aside.
With an electric mixer on high speed, beat butter, brown sugar
and egg until blended. Using a wooden spoon, stir in flour
mixture gradually. Finish mixing with hands, if necessary; stir
in almonds. Cover and chill dough for several hours. Roll out
dough thinly between sheets of wax paper; cut with cookie
cutters as desired. Arrange on greased baking sheets. Bake at
350 degrees until lightly golden but not overbaked, about
10 to 15 minutes. Makes about 3 dozen.

Use heart, diamond, club and spade cookie cutters to
cut out Speculaas...deliver with a package of new playing
cards to your favorite bridge partner.

German Lebkuchen

4 c. honey
11 c. all-purpose flour,
    divided
6 eggs
2-1/2 c. sugar
2 T. cinnamon
1 T. ground cloves
1 T. nutmeg

1 t. allspice
1/2 t. ground ginger
2 T. lemon juice
1 T. baking soda
Garnish: Powdered Sugar
    Frosting (page 29),
    whole almonds

Warm honey in a saucepan until thin; pour into a very large
mixing bowl. Stir in 6-1/4 cups flour; set aside. Beat eggs
until light and thick; add sugar and beat well. Stir in spices.
Mix lemon juice and baking soda; stir into mixture. Add
remaining flour; cover and chill. Drop by tablespoonfuls onto
lightly greased baking sheets. Bake at 350 degrees for 8 to
10 minutes. When cool, frost cookies; press one almond onto
each. Store in an airtight container. Makes 14 to 16 dozen.

Kitchen gadgets come in handy when decorating cookies.
Did you know you can squeeze dough through a garlic
press to make "hair" for a sweet gingerbread girl?

Gingerbread Scones

2 c. all-purpose flour	1 t. cinnamon
2 t. baking powder	7 T. butter, sliced
1/4 t. baking soda	1/3 c. molasses
1 t. ground ginger	1/3 c. milk

Combine flour, baking powder, baking soda and spices in a mixing bowl. Cut in butter with a pastry blender or 2 knives until crumbly. Combine molasses and milk; add to flour mixture, stirring just until moistened. Turn dough out onto a lightly floured surface; knead lightly 4 to 5 times. Divide dough in half; shape each portion into a ball. Pat each ball into a 5-inch circle on an ungreased baking sheet. Cut each circle into 6 wedges with a sharp knife; do not separate wedges. Bake at 425 degrees for 10 to 12 minutes, until lightly golden. Serve warm. Makes one dozen.

Hot spice-gingerbread, hot! Hot! All hot!
Come, buy my spice-gingerbread, smoking hot!
–18th-century gingerbread vendors' cry

Wild Blueberry Gingerbread Squares

1 teabag
1 c. boiling water
2-1/2 c. all-purpose flour
1 c. sugar
1 t. baking soda
1 t. salt
1/2 t. ground cloves

1/2 t. ground ginger
1/2 t. cinnamon
1/2 c. molasses
2 eggs, beaten
1/2 c. oil
1 c. blueberries

Place teabag in boiling water; let stand for 5 minutes. Mix together flour, sugar, baking soda, salt and spices in a large bowl. Discard teabag; stir hot tea, molasses, eggs and oil into flour mixture. Gently fold in berries. Pour into a greased and floured 13"x9" baking pan. Bake at 350 degrees for 30 to 35 minutes. Cut into squares. Makes 12 to 15 servings.

If cookies have been frozen ahead of time, it's a snap to make them taste fresh-baked in minutes. Place frozen cookies on a baking sheet and warm in a 300-degree oven for 3 to 5 minutes.

Ginger Meringue Cookies

2 egg whites
1/8 t. cream of tartar
1/3 c. sugar

1/4 t. almond extract
1 T. crystallized ginger,
　grated

Beat egg whites and cream of tartar with an electric mixer on high speed until soft peaks form. Gradually add sugar; beat until stiff peaks form. Fold in almond extract and ginger; drop by tablespoonfuls onto a parchment-lined baking sheet. Bake at 300 degrees for 40 minutes, or until crisp and dry; turn oven off. Do not remove meringues or open oven door for at least 2 hours. Remove from baking sheet; store in an airtight container. Makes about 2 dozen.

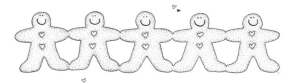

Cinnamon & Ginger Nuts

3 c. mixed nuts
1 egg white
1 T. orange juice
2/3 c. sugar

1 t. cinnamon
1/2 t. ground ginger
1/2 t. allspice
1/4 t. salt

Place nuts in a large mixing bowl; set aside. Whisk egg white and orange juice together until frothy; mix in remaining ingredients. Pour over nuts; mix thoroughly. Spread coated nuts onto an aluminum foil-lined baking sheet. Bake at 275 degrees for 45 minutes, stirring every 15 minutes. Cool; store in an airtight container. Makes 3 cups.

Chewy Molasses Dreams

3/4 c. shortening
1-1/2 c. sugar, divided
1 egg, beaten
1/3 c. molasses
2-1/3 c. all-purpose flour
2 t. baking soda

1/4 t. salt
2 t. cinnamon
2 t. nutmeg
2 t. ground ginger
1 t. ground cloves

Combine shortening, one cup sugar, egg and molasses; mix well. Blend in flour, baking soda, salt and spices. Shape into one-inch balls; roll in remaining sugar. Arrange on ungreased baking sheets; flatten slightly. Bake at 350 degrees for 7 to 8 minutes. Makes 3 to 4 dozen.

There's no easier gift bag than a classic brown paper lunch sack. Fill with treats, fold the top over, punch 2 holes and slide a peppermint stick through. You could even thread a licorice whip through the holes and tie into a bow!

Ginger-Coconut Papaya Tart

8-oz. pkg. cream cheese, softened
6 T. cream of coconut
3 T. sugar
1 c. sweetened flaked coconut, toasted and divided

1/4 c. crystallized ginger, chopped
9-inch pie crust, baked
2 papayas, peeled and thinly sliced
1/2 c. apricot preserves

Beat cream cheese with an electric mixer on low speed until smooth. Add cream of coconut, sugar, 3/4 cup coconut and ginger. Spread mixture in pie crust. Arrange papaya slices on top. In a small saucepan, heat preserves over low heat, stirring until melted; brush over papaya slices. Sprinkle remaining coconut over top. Chill for at least one hour, until firm. Makes 6 to 8 servings.

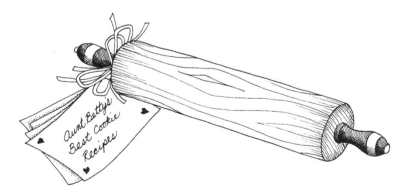

Aunt Betty's Best Cookie Recipes

A special gift to a new bride...pass down Grandma's rolling pin, along with some of her favorite recipes.

Orange-Ginger Spice Tea

2 c. water
4 thin slices fresh ginger,
    peeled
4-inch cinnamon stick,
    broken

8 whole cloves
2 teabags
1 c. orange juice
1 T. brown sugar, packed

Combine water and spices in a medium saucepan; bring to a boil. Remove from heat; add teabags and let stand for 5 minutes. Discard teabags. Stir in orange juice and brown sugar; heat through. Strain before serving. Makes 4 servings.

Take time to invite a girlfriend over for afternoon tea.
Serve freshly baked cookies with a steamy pot of
Orange-Ginger Spice Tea and spend time just catching up.

Gingerbread Custard Trifle

1/2 c. brown sugar, packed	1/2 t. salt
1/2 c. butter, softened	1 T. ground ginger
1 egg	1 c. hot water
1 c. molasses	8-oz. container frozen
2-1/2 c. all-purpose flour	whipped topping, thawed
2 t. baking powder	Garnish: 4 1.4-oz. toffee
1/2 t. baking soda	candy bars, chopped

With an electric mixer on low speed, gradually beat brown sugar into butter until light and fluffy. Add egg and molasses, beating well. Combine dry ingredients; add to butter mixture alternately with water, beating at low speed until blended. Pour into a greased 13"x9" baking pan. Bake at 350 degrees for 30 to 35 minutes, until a toothpick tests clean. Cool in pan on a wire rack; cut into cubes. Layer one-third of cubes in a 3-quart trifle bowl; top with one-third of cooled Vanilla Custard. Repeat layering twice, ending with custard. Chill. At serving time, spread whipped topping over trifle; garnish with chopped candy bars. Makes 10 servings.

Vanilla Custard:

1-1/3 c. sugar	5 c. milk
2/3 c. all-purpose flour	6 egg yolks, beaten
1/2 t. salt	1 T. vanilla extract

Combine sugar, flour and salt in a heavy saucepan; whisk in milk. Cook over medium heat, stirring constantly, until thickened and bubbly. Gradually stir one-quarter of hot mixture into egg yolks; add yolks to remaining hot mixture, stirring constantly. Cook and stir over medium heat for 3 minutes. Remove from heat; add vanilla. Cool to room temperature.

Spicy Gingerbread Cake

2 c. all-purpose flour
1 c. molasses
3/4 c. buttermilk
1/2 c. butter, softened
1/2 c. brown sugar, packed

1 t. baking soda
1/4 t. salt
1 t. cinnamon
1 t. ground ginger
1/4 t. ground cloves

Combine all ingredients in a large bowl. Beat with an electric mixer on low speed until well blended; beat on high speed for 2 minutes. Pour into a greased and floured 9"x9" baking pan. Bake at 325 degrees for 50 to 55 minutes, or until a toothpick inserted in the center comes out clean. Cool in pan on a wire rack for about 30 minutes. Cut into squares; serve warm. Makes 8 to 9 servings.

Hosting a dinner party? Stack a few cookies at each place setting and tie up with gingham ribbon...a sweet surprise for each guest.

Gingerbread Pancakes

1-1/2 c. all-purpose flour
1 t. baking powder
1/4 t. baking soda
1/4 t. salt
1 t. cinnamon
1/2 t. ground ginger

1 egg
1-1/4 c. milk
1/4 c. molasses
3 T. oil
Garnish: Lemon Sauce
(page 28)

Stir together flour, baking powder, baking soda, salt and spices in a small bowl; set aside. Beat together egg and milk in a large bowl; stir in molasses, then oil. Add flour mixture; stir just until combined. Lightly grease a griddle or skillet; heat until a drop of water dances on it. Pour batter by 1/4 cupfuls onto griddle; cook until puffed and bubbly at the edges. Turn and cook until other side is golden. Serve with warm Lemon Sauce. Makes about one dozen pancakes.

Why not get together with neighbors and have a potluck breakfast? Everyone brings their favorite dish...pancakes, waffles, sausage, bacon and you supply the coffee, tea, juice and cocoa. How fun!

Country Gingerbread Waffles

2 c. all-purpose flour
1/2 t. salt
1 t. cinnamon
1/2 t. ground ginger
1/2 c. butter
1 c. molasses

1-1/2 t. baking soda
1 c. light cream or sour milk
1 egg, beaten
Garnish: Chocolate Sauce
(page 28) or maple syrup

Stir together flour, salt and spices in a large bowl; set aside.
In a saucepan over low heat, melt butter and molasses
together. Remove from heat; beat in baking soda. Stir in cream
or milk and egg; add flour mixture. Pour batter by 1/4 cupfuls
onto a preheated, lightly greased waffle iron. Bake according to
manufacturer's directions. Serve with warm Chocolate Sauce
or maple syrup. Makes 6 to 8 waffles.

Spice a dish with love and it pleases every palate.

-Plautus

Gingerbread House Dough

2 c. shortening
2 c. molasses
2 c. sugar
2 t. baking soda
1 t. salt
2 T. cinnamon

2 t. ground cloves
1/2 t. ground ginger
9 to 10 c. all-purpose flour
Garnish: Royal Icing
(page 29)

In a 5-quart saucepan over low heat, cook shortening, molasses and sugar together until sugar dissolves, stirring constantly. Remove from heat; stir in baking soda, salt and spices. Gradually work in flour until a stiff dough forms; turn out onto a lightly floured surface and knead in as much remaining flour as possible while still maintaining a smooth consistency. Divide into 5 balls; wrap each in plastic wrap. Keep refrigerated until ready to use. Roll out each ball of dough 1/4-inch thick on a lightly floured surface. Cut into desired shapes; arrange on lightly greased baking sheets. Bake at 375 degrees for 10 to 14 minutes. Cool 3 to 4 minutes; remove to wire racks to cool completely. Assemble with Royal Icing. Makes one large gingerbread house.

A trip to the grocery store will yield lots of fun decorations for a gingerbread house...candy-coated chocolates, cinnamon candies, peppermints, cereal shapes and mini pretzels. Just use your imagination!

Soft Gingerbread Drop Cookies

1 c. margarine
1-1/2 c. brown sugar, packed
2 eggs, beaten
1/2 c. molasses
1 T. ground ginger
1-1/2 c. boiling water

5 c. all-purpose flour
2 t. baking powder
1-1/2 t. baking soda
1-1/2 t. salt
1 T. cinnamon
1 c. chopped walnuts

Blend margarine and sugar in a large bowl; stir in eggs.
Mix in molasses and ginger; stir in water. Combine remaining
ingredients except walnuts; add to margarine mixture. Fold
in nuts; cover and refrigerate dough at least 2 hours. Drop
by teaspoonfuls onto ungreased baking sheets. Bake at
425 degrees for 10 to 12 minutes. Makes about 6 dozen.

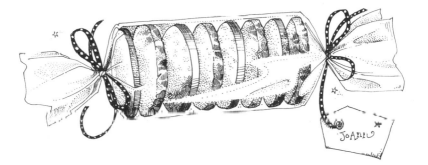

Roll stacks of cookies in clear or tinted cellophane and tie
the ends with curling ribbon...pile up in a pretty basket
as welcome favors for holiday visitors.

Lemon Sauce

1/2 c. sugar
1 T. cornstarch
1 c. hot water

2 T. butter
2 T. lemon juice

Combine sugar and cornstarch in a medium saucepan; gradually stir in water. Cook and stir over medium heat until thick and clear. Add butter and lemon juice; stir until butter melts. Keep warm.

Chocolate Sauce

2 c. water
1 c. sugar
1/2 c. baking cocoa
2 T. cornstarch

1 t. salt
2 t. vanilla extract
2 T. butter

Bring water to a boil in a small saucepan. Add sugar, cocoa, cornstarch and salt. Cook over medium heat, stirring constantly, until mixture comes to a boil. Remove from heat; add vanilla and butter. Stir until smooth.

Mix & match! Lemon and chocolate sauces are yummy with gingerbread cakes, waffles and pancakes. Powdered sugar frosting is a good all-purpose cookie frosting, while royal icing dries "hard"...perfect for fancy designs.

Powdered Sugar Glaze

1 c. powdered sugar
1-1/2 T. milk

1/2 t. vanilla extract

Whisk ingredients together to a drizzling consistency;
if needed, add more milk. Makes about one cup.

Powdered Sugar Frosting

1 c. powdered sugar
3-1/2 t. milk
1/4 t. vanilla extract

Optional: food coloring
2 t. corn syrup

Stir together powdered sugar, milk, vanilla and food coloring,
if using, in a small bowl. Add corn syrup; stir until smooth and
glossy. If too thick, add a little more corn syrup. Use frosting
immediately; let cookies dry completely before stacking.
Makes about one cup.

Royal Icing

4 c. powdered sugar
3 pasteurized egg whites

1/2 t. cream of tartar
Optional: food coloring

Combine all ingredients except food coloring in a large bowl.
Beat with an electric mixer on high speed for 7 to 10 minutes.
If desired, divide into several small bowls; add food coloring
to each. Use immediately. Makes about 2 cups.

Let the kids get creative with cookie frosting!
Set out a small new paintbrush for each color.

Decorating
GINGERBREAD
COOKIES
in a...

SNAP!

It's easy and fun! Set out frosting along with small bowls of sprinkles, colored sugar and small candies and...

make a face!
with raisins, red cinnamon candies and gumdrops

pipe it!
with royal icing
in a pastry cone

swirl it!
with frosting and
a mini spatula

sparkle it!
with sparkly
sanding sugar

dip it!
in melted
white chocolate

stencil it!
with powdered sugar
and a doily

USE YOUR
IMAGINATION*
HERE!

Fresh from the Kitchen of

Baked for YOU with L♥VE!

copy, color, SHARE!

Put together a clever gift package...arrange lots of gingerbread cookies on a vintage pie plate, then tie up with tulle. So pretty!

Did you know?
European bakers have been making gingerbread for more than 500 years! Lebkuchen, Pepparkakor and Speculaas are some of the oldest kinds.

"Had I but one penny in the world, thou shouldst have it for Ginger-bread!"

–William Shakespeare–

Index